T0400125

I Know the Rules!

I RAISE MY HAND!

By Bray Jacobson

Gareth Stevens
PUBLISHING

Please visit our website, www.garethstevens.com. For a free color catalog of all our high-quality books, call toll free 1-800-542-2595 or fax 1-877-542-2596.

Library of Congress Cataloging-in-Publication Data

Names: Jacobson, Bray, author.
Title: I raise my hand! / Bray Jacobson.
Description: Buffalo, New York : Gareth Stevens Publishing, [2024] |
    Series: I know the rules! | Includes index.
Identifiers: LCCN 2022051473 (print) | LCCN 2022051474 (ebook) | ISBN
    9781538286654 (library binding) | ISBN 9781538286647 (paperback) | ISBN
    9781538286661 (ebook)
Subjects: LCSH: Courtesy–Juvenile literature. | Social skills in
    children–Juvenile literature. | Children–Conduct of life–Juvenile
    literature.
Classification: LCC BJ1533.C9 J33 2024 (print) | LCC BJ1533.C9 (ebook) |
    DDC 177/.1–dc23/eng/20230120
LC record available at https://lccn.loc.gov/2022051473
LC ebook record available at https://lccn.loc.gov/2022051474

Published in 2024 by
Gareth Stevens Publishing
2544 Clinton Street
Buffalo, NY 14224

Copyright © 2024 Gareth Stevens Publishing

Designer: Claire Wrazin
Editor: Kristen Nelson

Photo credits: cover, pp. 5, 7, 9, 11 (main), 17 wavebreakmedia/Shutterstock.com; pp. 11 (pass), 24 (pass) Stephen Coburn/Shutterstock.com; p. 11 (arrow) Lyudmyla Ishchenko/Shutterstock.com; p. 13 Monkey Business Images/Shutterstock.com; p. 15 UfaBizPhoto/Shutterstock.com; pp. 19, 21, 23 fizkes/Shutterstock.com; p. 23 sivilla/Shutterstock.com; p. 24 (nurse) Pixel-Shot/Shutterstock.com.

Printed in the United States of America

CPSIA compliance information: Batch #CSGS24: For further information contact Gareth Stevens, at 1-800-542-2595.

Find us on

Contents

I raise my hand
at school.
It is a rule.

Mrs. Patel asks
a question.
Josh raises his hand.
She calls on him.

Gabrielle needs the bathroom pass.
She raises her hand.

9

Mrs. Patel gives her the pass.

Mr. Gerrity has jobs
for the class.
Lana raises her hand.
She wants to help.

She puts away
the books.

Sylvester feels sick.
He raises his hand.
The nurse helps him.

Jace raises his hand at home.
It shows his dad he needs something.

Dad is on the phone.
Jace needs help.
Jace raises his hand.

His dad takes a break
from his call.

Words to Know

nurse

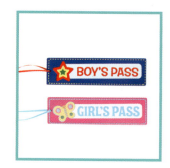

pass

Index